WORDS FOR TIRED HEARTS

Logan Duane

Copyright © 2022 Logan Duane

All rights reserved. No part of this book may be reproduced
or used in any manner without the prior written permission of the copyright owner,
except for the use of brief quotations in a book review.

To request permissions, contact the author at
loganduanepoetry@gmail.com

Instagram:
@logan.duane.poetry

*For those of you
who feel like
you've never been heard;
I hear you.*

*For the parts of me
that I've lost
on this journey;
I miss you.*

Content Warning:

This book contains depictions of abuse, suicide, sexual assault, body dysmorphia, eating disorders, violence, and depression.
Reader discretion is advised.

Your mental health matters; always take care of yourself.

CONTENTS

TIRED HEARTS .... PG. 6

WANDERING SOULS .... PG. 59

RESTLESS MINDS .... PG. 103

TIRED HEARTS

Content Warning: abuse, depression, sexual assault, manipulation

Just because my heart
beats
does not mean that
it's alive

you can't destroy something
over and over again
and expect it not to
die inside.

-{for tired hearts}

I lived for you,
and I will die
aching for you to come back to me.

-{you were the only home I've ever known}

I loved you
just long enough
for it to destroy me
when you left.

You loved me
just long enough
to make leaving
look effortless.

I'm afraid of
living alone

but I am far more afraid
of what might happen
if I choose to
stay here instead.

-*{I have to break free}*

Maybe we were never
meant to be
together
like we once thought.

Maybe we were
broken
from the start.

We never had any issues until
I started standing up
for myself.

I guess it's a sign that you never
really loved me,
you only loved
my obedience.

You forgot how
to love me

and then begged
for me to stay
when I chose to
love myself instead.

Winter will never feel
colder

than the space
between these sheets.

You make me feel
fucking crazy

and you do it
with a smile
on your face.

-*{gaslighter}*

In the absence of love
we chose pain

and that's the biggest
heartbreak of all.

Some people are only
meant to be
a moment in time
despite the promise
of forever.

-*{you are my favorite memory}*

I shouldn't flinch at the thought of
sex,
but I do

and I hope you fall asleep at night
knowing it's because of
you.

You became the very thing
that you promised
to protect me from.

-*{trust issues}*

We are just two
strangers

who used to be
completely in love.

We are just two
souls

who wander this house
trying desperately to make it

a home again.

I used to worship the ground
you walked on

now I am begging for you
to just be kind to me.

Tell me why
I long for you to
love me
when you've proven
you don't care.

Tell me why I ache
for you to do what's right
when I know
you'll never change.

Tell me why I create
fake images of you
in my brain, wishing for
a version of you
that only exists in my dreams.

I never asked for much,
only for your support.
Tell me why
that's so hard to give.

You watered
every other flower
but me
and then wondered why I
wilted.

-{was I not beautiful enough?}

I could scream

I could whisper

You wouldn't hear me
either way.

Love doesn't live
in this house anymore.

The walls reek of
lies and deceit.

The floorboards creak
under the weight of
the sadness and despair
that lingers in the air.

Memories of us
collect dust in the cabinets.

Love doesn't live
in our hearts anymore.

We are trying to ignite
an eternal flame
with nothing but
ashes.

-{the death of forever}

You don't make me feel loved,

you make me feel convenient.

One day,
I will find the courage
to leave.

And when I do,

I hope your heart
bleeds
until your veins run dry and shrivel.

I hope your brain
melts
from the heat of the rage you carry within.

I hope you fucking
rot
from the inside out, until you're nothing but
dust.

You will cry
at my funeral
as if
you aren't the devil
that came and
sucked the life
straight from my lungs.

Home
feels so comfortable,
and so foreign
all at once.

-*{growing apart}*

I still have lots of
hopes and dreams

you're just no longer
part of them.

You used to kiss me like
the stars
kiss the surface of
a still river
in the dead of night.

You used to love me like
the sun
loves to glow in the bends of
a still river
during golden hour.

Now you've left me wondering
when our river
ran dry.

Were we ever
really in love

or were we
bound together
by trauma
and late night sex?

I lie mangled in a pile
on your unmade bed
vulnerability pouring from my veins
and fear trickling down my face.

You had me convinced
that this is love

but now I'm starting
to rethink.

You make
blaming me
look so damn easy.

I opened up doors
that should have remained
closed

and now I'm trapped
in an empty room
with a monster who
had me convinced
that he was different.

I ache to be
someone
worth loving.

I obeyed

you destroyed

you called it balance

I called it hell

There's something sinister inside of me
that tells me that
I should meet your anger
with twice as much rage.
I should fight fire
with gasoline.
I should use words
that cut deeper than yours.

-*{it's the only way you'll listen to me}*

When you look at me,

do you see the
woman you love

or do you see
a body to fuck?

Everything I say
is used against me
so I guess I'll just stay silent.

You'll spin some tale
about things I
never said
and make everyone believe
I'm the bad guy

and I'll have no choice
but to let them
believe it

because who wants to listen
to the bad guy
anyway?

Before I knew it
I'd given myself
to a man with
a god complex
and an affinity
for vulnerable women.

You taught me that
sex
is a weapon,
and that my own
body
is a punishment.

I hope you receive
the same kind of energy
that you put out

and I hope that
the next girl
treats you the way
you treated me.

The older I get,
the more wounds I find
hidden among the depths
of my soul.

Each one of them
spells out
your name.

Good deeds
that are used against you
are not good deeds at all.

They're tools
they create
just to make you feel small.

Rely on
no one
except yourself.

-{self preservation}

She showed me
all of the ways
that love can grow
when you allow it
to.

-*{the me after you}*

I will grow

I will heal

I will change

and it'll kill you
to watch me thrive.

-*{the best revenge}*

I want to believe you
when you tell me

I'm beautiful.

You remind me
of what it's like
to fall in love
all over again.

I presented you
a blackened heart
that he didn't want,
and you caressed it
in your gentle hands
like I'd given you
the entire world.

I promise to love you
in ways that
I was never loved.

In that moment
I wanted nothing more
than to live
forever.

-{*immortality*}

You rekindled the
fire in my soul
with a single breath.

Take my hand
and walk among
the stars with me.

-*{I'd go anywhere with you}*

Every living creature
on this planet
deserves love,
compassion,
kindness
and respect -

including yourself.

-*{affirmations}*

Never stop spreading
empathy and love,
even when
your heart feels
tired and hollow.

-*{you make the world beautiful, darling}*

WANDERING SOULS

Content Warning: suicide, depression, mental illness, death

I'm not sure
where I belong

but I have never felt
like it was
here.

-{*for wandering souls*}

I sleep with
my arms strapped to my bed
so I'm not tempted
to fly away
into my dreams.

-{grounded}

I am grieving
for the person
that I used to be.

-*{I want her to come back to me}*

Some days, it feels like
I might fall
to the center of the Earth
and succumb to
scalding iron and flames
if I can't let go
of this baggage I carry around.

When I look in the mirror,
I see a girl who
has learned to
hate all of the things
that make me who
I am.

-*{stolen identity}*

I'm just a
lost heart

floating aimlessly
in the clouds

with no idea
where it's supposed to land.

I hardly know my
own name
these days

my hopes and dreams
have been
overshadowed
by wounds that I can't heal

and I'm so
out of touch
with my conscience
that even reality
feels like a fantasy.

I died
long ago.

My empty body now
roams around
day after day

waiting for the
soul I lost
to reunite with
my decaying corpse.

My greatest fear is that
I will become
everything that I despise
just to make others happy.

A child with
a thirst for knowledge

crushed under the weight of it all

crumbled under the pressure.

-*{a tragedy}*

If you're reading this,

it's
time
to
come
home.

-*{a letter to my sanity}*

Some memories feel
better
if I leave them
between the four walls
of my childhood bedroom.

A fairy with
no wings
just walks
among the trees
with no purpose.

-*{I've lost my ability to fly}*

I'm standing at the edge
of a dead-end road
with my head turned
up toward the stars
desperate for one of them
to show me where to go next.

Maybe I'm not tired
of being alive.

Maybe I'm just tired of
not knowing who I am.

I feel trapped
in a life
that I never
asked for.

I don't want to live
in a mind
that doesn't feel like mine.

I'm a stranger
in my own body

while someone else
controls my brain
and I just have to live with the consequences.

I've been searching for myself
on roads paved
by other hands.
I've been following road signs
pointing me in directions
that mold me into a
perfect woman

but that's not me

and now I'm lost
on a lonely back road
with no concept of
who I am.

The things that
used to make me smile
feel like nothing
but distant memories
with no hope
of ever returning to me.

How am I
supposed to love
a person that
I don't know?

-*{love yourself}*

It's tempting to
fall in love with
gravity

and let her teach me
how to
free fall.

I will no longer
dance
with death

I will
embrace it.

There was a time
in my life
that I lived freely.

I loved how I wanted.
I loved who I wanted.
I was proud to be
who I was.

Until you.

You broke me
to the depths of my core

stripped me down to
nothing
and stole each part of my
identity.

You sculpted me into
a brand new person
that I don't recognize anymore

and now I lay awake at night
longing for the girl
who felt
free.

Somewhere
out there,
there's a version of me
that's at peace.

I envy her.

I possess a
painful desire
to abandon all that is
comfortable

and chase a
brand new beginning.

-{greener grasses}

Tell me -

how fast do I
have to run

to finally start
going somewhere?

Each time I
build myself back up,
you find a
crack in my foundation,

and use it to
rip me down
again.

I'm really fucking
sick and tired
of feeling like I have to
thank people
just for having me in their lives.

-{worthy}

If each new day
is a gift

then why don't I
feel like
celebrating?

-{unwanted presents}

I am
haunted
by the ghost of the girl
that I murdered
to become someone
that I hate.

-*{I miss who I used to be}*

Don't want to live
Don't want to die

just constant purgatory
in my mind.

When I was younger,
I was sure that
after 18
my insufferable illnesses
wouldn't hurt me anymore.

And maybe that's because
everyone had me convinced
that I was childish
for feeling what I was feeling
and acting how I was acting.

I used to tell myself that
if I could make it to 18,
I would be free.

If I could make it to 18,
I wouldn't have to experience those
childish things anymore
and maybe I could finally
move on with my life.

Oh, how wrong I was.

Suck the life from
my lungs
and leave me to
drown in emptiness.

Tear the heart
from my chest
and feed it
to the wolves.

Steal the thoughts
from my mind
and bury them
six feet under.

Pick away
at my soul
until I am nothing but
a skeleton

so you can
create a version of me
who I can't
recognize.

Everything seems
so trivial
when you go to war
with yourself
just to wake up
in the morning.

He saw me coming
from miles away,
a vulnerable girl
who had lost her way.

I trusted him
for a moment, I did.
Couldn't see past his smile
where all his hatred hid.

I give everyone
so much of myself
that I'm left with
a pile of crumbs
to fuel my entire existence.

-{starving}

I only wish that my life will end
before I lose what's left
of my mind.

This world will steal
every ounce of
creativity
that I have left
if I allow it.

-{thievery}

My brain is
a funeral home
for serotonin.

My body is
a morgue
for hopeful hearts.

When did I become too busy to
take care of myself?

When did waking up
become a chore,
and not a new adventure to be had?

When is it my turn
to be happy?

I would give anything
to find a way
to heal

without destroying those around me.

I ran away from my life
and waited for someone
to come find me

but incidentally
found myself
instead.

Let go of
everything you've
ever known
and venture into
something exciting,
something new.

Release yourself
from the shackles of
your past
and embrace
freedom.

-{let your soul wander}

RESTLESS MINDS

Content Warning: suicide, depression, mental illness, eating disorders, substance use, abuse, body dysmorphia

If I could just
slow down,
take a breath,
and fill my chest
with something that doesn't
feel like lead

then maybe I could
think clearly again.

-*{for restless minds}*

I would serve you
my head
on a silver platter

just so you could
have a taste
of what it's like
to live inside of it
for just a moment.

I want to tell you
that I'm happy,
but you'd see the darkness
behind the facade.

I wish I could tell you
that it's gotten better,
but I've run out of the strength
to lie.

I just want to live
without waiting
to die.

Believe it or not,
I had happiness
once.

The universe came
and ripped it from my hands
just as fast as
it had been given to me.

And once it was gone,

the pain of my sadness
hurt far more
than it ever had before.

-*{double-edged sword}*

I am a
missed medication away
from irreversible
insanity.

Forgive me for
my frustration;

I've been a
revolving door
of psychiatric medications
for as long as I can remember.

I'm still stick,

but I can tell you every
unwanted side effect
of each SSRI,
antipsychotic,
or off label medication
you want to throw at me.

Forgive me, doctor.
I just don't think they make
a medication

that'll fix me.

-{a letter to my psychiatrist}

a sink full of dirty dishes
sweat stained sheets
matted hair
takeout boxes in the folds of my bed
missed calls
missed messages
skipping work just to lay in bed
tears on my pillows
letters on my nightstand

-{it's getting bad again}

In elementary school, we learned that

what
goes
up,
must
always
come
down

and I never knew if my teachers were
referring to physics
or emotions.

-*{bipolar}*

I feel myself
slipping
into bad habits again

but that's just how it goes
you know?

and the fucked up part is that
it's comforting,
because it's the only time
that my mind
stops spinning.

Self medicating
won't fix it

but it will
allow me to forget

even if just
for a moment.

Sometimes I can't tell
if it's better to remember

or to maintain my sobriety.

-*{relapse}*

Confront your problems
or let them eat you alive

either way,
they won't disappear.

-{lessons learned the hard way}

How am I supposed to heal
if I am
addicted
to destroying myself?

-*{pity party}*

Anger and frustration
bubble at my fingertips
begging to come out through
my hands

but instead
they come out as
hot tears
that run down my face.

-{angry crier}

My hands are wrapped
so tightly around my own neck

that I'm not sure
I'll survive for much longer.

-{self destruct}

Today,
I just want to
drive my car
straight into the ocean
with the windows up
and the doors locked
and let all of my problems
drown
with the rest of my body and soul.

Our house
looks like a castle
to those who pass by

but these four walls
contain a sadistic hell
where little girls
go to die.

-{home sweet home}

How can two people
remember the same man
so differently?

-*{I protected you from everything I didn't want you to see}*

When you take off
your rose-colored glasses,

you'll finally be able to see
the darkness and turmoil
that exist in your environment.

You'll wonder how
you didn't see it before now.

You'll feel things
you've never felt before.

Everything you've ever known
will melt in front of your eyes

and you'll sell your soul
to the devil himself
to spend one more day
in a rose-colored world.

Life is a cruel game
that I don't want to
fucking play anymore

my clothes are suffocating me
and my skin is too tight
the air is too heavy in my lungs
and my surroundings are too loud
so loud that each noise bounces around in my head
and bounces and bounces and bounces
as if a toddler is using my brain like a trampoline
and although my eyes are open
I can't see where I'm going
everything is a blur that rushes by
I feel like I'm screaming
but my mouth remains closed
and among the chaos
all of my thoughts are lost

-{overstimulated}

I'm addicted to

throwing matches

into a fire that
will continue to
burn me

until the day that I

parish.

I chase numbers on the scale
like today will be the day
that I'm allowed
to love myself.

Do you know how
truly frightening it is
to walk through life
without knowing what
your own body
really looks like?

-{perspective}

The fucked up part of it all
is that everyone tells you

how beautiful you look

when you've missed a few
too many meals.

-{feed the disorder}

If you don't
love yourself now
you won't love yourself
when you're thinner.

Do you care
about how many calories
you consume

or is it the only thing
you have control of?

-*{food for thought}*

Maybe if I hide my body
behind layers of
oversized clothes,
they won't see what I
really look like.

And maybe if I make the first joke
about my weight,
I can protect my heart
from the targeted "big girl" comments.

Or maybe if I tell them that I'm sick,
I can stay home
where no one can look at me.

Maybe if I lost weight
I would be happy.

I just want to be happy.

In a room filled
with nothing but
open air and silence

I'm still unable to sit
comfortably
in my own body.

I spend so much time
trying to be thin
that I forget
to live.

Nothing feels safe anymore

food
clothes
family
friends

everything is an enemy.

I feel so alone.

-*{isolation}*

What would be
so bad
about giving yourself permission
to eat whatever
you want to eat?

What would happen
if you let go
of the voice in your head
telling you that
eating will make you
unlovable?

What would happen
if you stopped fearing food
and used it as a tool
to fuel your precious body?

What would happen
if you decided to love yourself?

-*{take back control}*

Just remember that
diet culture
wants you to hate yourself.

They make money
on your suffering
while living in your head
for free.

-*{fuck 'em}*

It's not your fault
that you have
internalized fatphobia,

but it is your responsibility
to overcome it
and heal your way of thinking.

-{unlearning diet culture}

Step away from the mirror, darling.

You're only
hurting yourself.

It is impossible to
heal
when you're surrounded by
people who only love you
when you're wounded.

-*{find people who always love you}*

Stop going to war
with a body
who fights so hard
for you.

-*{inner peace}*

Let yourself
change.

-*{grow without them}*

You deserve peace
after 23 years
of torturing yourself
and hating the body
you're in.

I can no longer
protect you
from things you're
not willing
to acknowledge.

-*{you're too far gone}*

You told us that
the smaller we are
the better we look

the more calories we restrict
the more successful we are

skipping meals was okay
as long as we were losing weight

diet trends are cool
and our bodies are shameful.

You taught us that
diets have no age restrictions
and little girls should be thin

our value is based on a number
and we should hide our insecurities

beauty is essential
and intelligence is useless.

You bred a generation
of eating disorders
and broken girls

that grew up to be women
that have to clean up your mess

for our daughters.

-*{mothers}*

You've become so good at
hiding the pain

that you've forgotten how
truly liberating it is
to let it go.

-{*free yourself*}

Never let your voice be silenced by those
who feel that they have the right
to control you.

Never let a man
assert power over you
simply because he is a man.

Strong women are the future
of this world.

One day,
you'll wake up
and smile
at the sun.

-*{it won't always be raining}*

The child in me
is desperate
to find peace

and I know that
I'm the only one
who can give her what she needs.

I'm not sure what that is yet,
but I am going to
figure it out

for her.

-{we both deserve to rest}

Made in the USA
Las Vegas, NV
05 September 2023

77082479R00090